Daily Devotionals

Insight for Living

Olu & Vicki David

Revealed Word Publishers

Unless otherwise indicated, all scripture quotations are taken from the King James Version of the Bible.

Devotionals -Insight for living

ISBN-978-1-257-65116-0

Published in CANADA by the Revealed Word Publishers

TO ORDER FOR PREVIOUS, CURRENT OR NEXT MONTH'S EDITION PLEASE CONTACT US AT :

10-377 Mackenzie Avenue Ajax, On L1S 2G2

Tel: 1-905-426-4110 Fax: 1-905-720-2442

E-mail: info@rhomi.org

Website: www.rhomi.org, www.rhomi.org/2, www.chogi.org

Strengthen your spirit. Think the Word.

Charge your body and enjoy the daily

victories.

DAILY DEVOTIONALS

JUNE 2011

……. These are extracts from the daily devotional postings from the notes on ***Pastor Olu & Vicki David facebook*** page designed to give insight to the Kingdom way of living, providing hope, instructions and strength to deal with day -to- day living experiences and challenges.

Your mind will be prepared, your heart refreshed and your feelings aligned with the Spirit of the Word of God.

Enjoy reading and meditating.

Let us know how you are blessed. Write or contact us @ info @rhomi.org

Daily Devotionals and Insights for Living June 2011

WE HAVE COME TO THE FATHER
DAY 1

Jesus saith unto him, I am the way, the truth, and the life: no man cometh unto the Father, but by me.
John 14:6
We have been saved to have a very deep intimate relationship with the Father. The life of Jesus Christ was designed to reveal God to us as our Father. When God saved Israel out of Egypt, He had to remind them that He brought them to HIMSELF
Ye have seen what I did unto the Egyptians, and how I bare you on eagles' wings, and brought you unto myself.
Exodus 19:4
And Moses brought forth the people out of the camp to meet with God; and they stood at the nether part of the mount.
Exodus 19:17
Israel was set free to serve Him and worship Him (Exodus 8:1). The labour of bondage and affliction prevented genuine worship. Deliverance is guaranteed if your aim is to worship Him. Your freedom is to worship Him; your promised land is a place of worship. We have not been saved to have things/materials. It's not about enjoying this world or this life, having husband and children. The primary reason for your call to salvation is to be with Him, to worship Him, serve Him, in a very

deep intimate relationship. When Jesus called the apostles, He called them to be with Him first (Mark 3:13-14), before He sent them out. The activities, ministry, and other things, even life, come secondary. The fulfillment of those is a product of solid relationship with God. Nothing you have or He gave you should take His place in your life. You are not saved for tasks, refused to be entangled again with the yoke of bondage and activities. In Christ you are free to worship, you have come to the Father. Amen

Other's Comment

Angel David-Yes I was listening to last year's message (May 27) and one thing that stood out to me was John 17:18-24. Jesus was praying that we be one with Him and the Father as He is one with God. When we got saved we were called to obtain GLORY

Own Comment

____

____

____

____

____

____

____

____

____

____

____

____

____

____

____

____

Prayer:

Dear Father, thank You for setting me free so I can worship You. I have come to You Father and I am dwelling in Your presence. I receive grace to stay bondage free and yoke free. I shall not be entangled or hindered in Jesus' name.

RUNNING THE RACE
DAY 2

Wherefore seeing we also are compassed about with so great a cloud of witnesses, let us lay aside every weight, and the sin which doth so easily beset us, and let us run with patience the race that is set before us,

Looking unto Jesus the author and finisher of our faith; who for the joy that was set before him endured the cross, despising the shame, and is set down at the right hand of the throne of God.

Hebrews 12:1-2

Your lifetime is a race; you have a race to run, and you have to run it with endurance, looking unto Jesus. You have to run it alone, avoiding distractions. Many have been sidetracked, stopped or discouraged in running the race before them. They take their eyes off Jesus, become impatient, look for support and most times are heavily distracted. Some go into hiding, drop the ball and try all they can to get out of the race.

The evil world system programs us for competition from the day we were born. From home our parents put pressure on us to be better than the other kids, while in school we're induced by peers and teachers to strive to be better than the others. And the media is ever putting before us the image of other people to model our lives after. It is so easy to be drawn into the competition of life, trying to be somebody else, or better than some others.

We define ourselves by other people's standards, whom sometimes we judge to be more talented, gifted, successful, or more beautiful. We grow day by day, living with temptation to compare ourselves with somebody else and sometimes we feel inferior or superior. Because we have to catch up with our neighbors or some other guy, we impose undue pressures on ourselves that sometimes make our lives so stressful. The unfortunate thing is we never know when this will end, it's like we're entrapped in a cycle of competition all our lives, leaving pains, shortcomings, and a vacuum behind.

Beloved, aren't you glad that in Christ you have no competitor in the race before you? The beautiful thing about this race is that you are the only one on the track. The only condition to win and to get the prize is to finish it. What freedom to know that you don't have to keep up with anybody, be anybody, do what anybody is doing, envy what anybody has or does not have. You can be grateful for where you are, who you are, what you have and where you are going to. If your car will not break down, and you will not stop refueling, you will surely get there. Every child of God is a winner in Christ.

Own Comment

____

____

____

____

____

____

____

____

____

Prayer

Dear Father, I thank You for empowering me for the race that is set before me. Christ is my focus and goal, my Starter and Finisher, and in Him I am a winner. I shall not be weighed down or distracted in my race of faith.

WHO ARE YOU LISTENING TO?
DAY 3

While he yet spake, there came from the ruler of the synagogue's house certain which said, Thy daughter is dead: why troublest thou the Master any further?

As soon as Jesus heard the word that was spoken, he saith unto the ruler of the synagogue, Be not afraid, only believe
Mark 5:35-36
(...as soon as Jesus heard the word that was spoken...)
Jairus sought for prayer, came to Jesus for help like a man in church believing God for a breakthrough. His daughter was chronically sick; so much time was spent attending to someone else on the way or some other issues and while still at prayers or in church with Jesus, the worst news came from a member of his household "Your case has just gone from bad to worse..." they said. Haven't you noticed that it's much easier for people around you to rush to give you the bad news but may not be eager to go to prayers with you. You will always find company to mourn with, or comfort you when things go worse, but few to stand with you in prayer or go to church with you in order to prevent the days of mourning.
The world's government and financial system is designed as a cure program to attend to breakdowns, failures, sickness etc rather than prevention. They pay more to medical doctors treating cancer than teachers teaching healthy eating habits. Less is invested in encouraging parents to spend more time with their kids at home than to prosecutors, lawyers and judges who put them in jail. The bad news came to Jairus right in Christ's presence. What on earth do you think was going through his mind? But I thank God Jesus was listening and He responded. Jesus is listening and is responding today to all the negative and hopeless news, evil and depressing reports we hear daily from doctors, media, friends, family members or bank statements etc. (...and he said be not afraid, only believe...) It is not yet over.
Jairus had a choice to make;
1 Listen to Jesus or get up and leave

2 Listen to Jesus or get up and blame
3 Listen to Jesus or be discouraged and shut down everybody
4 Listen to Jesus or leave to go home to bury his daughter.
But he chose to listen to Jesus (V. 38). Beloved will you please get up and go back to church. Dust your bible start listening.

Own Comment

____
____
____
____
____
____
____
____
____

Prayer
Dear Father, I thank You for being with me at all times. Because You are with me I shall not fear nor will I listen to voices of doubt and discouragement. I choose to listen to the voice of the Lord and it shall be as He told me in Jesus name.Amen.

WHAT TO DO WITH CARES AND CONCERNS-DAY 4

Casting all your care upon him; for he careth for you. 1 Peter 5:7

Beloved, we have to learn how to leave our worries, and concerns, and troubles on the Lord 's Table. This is one thing so difficult for us to do because many of us are trained never to trust anyone with the responsibility of solving our problems. Our experiences in life have shown us that we need to do something to get the problem solved. We wake up every day to realize that nobody really cares unless we do. While some of us just love to worry or like the idea of self accomplishment, so we just can't let anybody else handle our issues for us. Some of us love God and Christ so much that we think that there are some issues we shouldn't bother them with; we think some things are our responsibility and we shouldn't bother the Lord with them, while some of us just simply find it so hard to trust the Lord.

Beloved, the heart of trust is more than just an act; it is the essence of a believer. Simple trust in the Lord is the singular key to free your mind and soul from all the worries and cares of this life. The Lord Jesus cares for us so much, that He is willing to be our load carrier. He's not differentiating the loads; He's concerned about them all, whether big or small.

Trust releases the saving strength of His right hand (Psalm 20:6-7). Trust releases the shield and protection of the Almighty over us (Psalm 91:2-6) Trust activates the presence of the angels around us (Psalm 125:1-2, 34:7-8). Absolute, 100% casting your cares unto the Lord is the guarantee for super spiritual victories in every issue of your life.

Beloved, start casting your cares today, stop worrying, go to sleep, rejoice; your cares are being handled by the Lord. It shall be well. Amen.

Own Comment

____

____

____

____

____

____

____

____

____

Prayer

Dear Father, I thank You for caring for me tenderly as Your sheep. I put my trust and hope in You Lord therefore I shall not be ashamed. I leave my worries, cares and concerns on the Your table because I am certain You are taking care of them all. Amen.

HOW DO YOU REPSOND TO HEAT?
DAY 5

But the more they afflicted them, the more they multiplied and grew. And they were grieved because of the children of Israel. Exodus 1:12

I read a story recently of the response of a potato, an egg, and coffee beans to heat. When a potato boils in water, it gets softened up but leaves little or no effect on the water around it. And the same goes for the egg, when it boils in the water, the inside hardens up, the shell remains the same and leaves no effect on the water around it. But not so with the coffee beans; the more heat it gets, the more it changes the colour of the water around it to look like itself and fills the air with its aroma.

The water represents the situation around us or wherever the heat comes through to us. The key difference among the three is the strength; the ability to withstand heat and how it uses heat to change its environment.

Are you a potato, an egg, or coffee beans? Some people are like eggs with a soft inside that gets hardened up on the inside, become cold, untrusting, withdrawn, and sometimes grow very mean and become tough when faced with heat, and then they blame their bad experiences and circumstances of their life for their coldness.

Some are like the potato, which look tough and strong before the heat, but in no time due to trying situations, get weakened, softened up, and begin to run about and around like weaklings; sometimes they lay back and are unwilling to advance or try anything new because of fear.

But the man of love and strength is like a coffee bean that influences his environment using the heat from it. It's like an inflated ball, the harder you bounce it against a rock, the higher it goes.

Beloved, God is your strength, it doesn't matter what you're going through; the persecutions, opposition, troubles that may come from the environment around you, you are not breaking because of the love of God and the strength of the living God within you. The same troubles, afflictions, are what you need to change the environment around you, emitting the fragrance of His grace and knowledge. We glory in tribulation, we use persecutions; the trial of our faith is more precious than gold.

That the trial of your faith, being much more precious than of gold that perisheth, though it be tried with fire, might be found unto praise and honour and glory at the appearing of Jesus Christ: 1 Peter 1:7

The bible says count it all joy (James 1:2). What you call trouble is what the heavens call training and open doors. Be strong in the Lord. Amen

Other's Comment

Yvette Cameron-One thing I can say heat (difficult circumstances and situations) has done for me is to make me better. You can either be made bitter or better by it. I have found that it is a choice you have to consciously make whether or not you will benefit from it but with Christ as the third man in the fire there is grace, strength and power to endure and come out without even the smell of smoke on your clothes.

Own Comment

Prayer

Dear Father, I thank you for putting Your love in my heart. I declare I am strong by the Holy Spirit in my inner man. I am affecting and influencing my environment. I am not going down or out in Jesus name.

WHO WE ARE
DAY 6

There be many that say, Who will shew us any good? LORD, lift thou up the light of thy countenance upon us

Psalm 4:6

Many of us have misinterpreted God's plan because of our experiences. We wish to go to heaven, and we're waiting for the day we're leaving the earth to go to heaven. But as we take another look at the word, we see that when Jesus came, He **brought** the kingdom **to earth**, (Matthew 12:28). And also in the Lord's prayer, He says in Matthew 6:10 "Thy kingdom **come,** thy will be done **on earth** as it is in heaven". So God is not so much interested in having us leave the earth and escape to heaven, but rather we are to bring heaven to earth.

What we sons of God represent to the world, and to the lost, is the power/ability to enter into the temple. We are a bridge through Jesus to God, as Christ was and is a bridge to God for us. When our father David asked God in Psalms 4:6 "who will show us any good?" God's answer was Jesus, He is the light of God's countenance. And we likewise are the light of Jesus' countenance, and through our life, our words, and actions people see Jesus. We are the light they will see and either despise or accept.

We don't need to hide from that "ungodly" person anymore in trying to preserve our godliness; that's in God's hand. Instead we show that ungodly person our godliness. And if they receive us, then they just received Christ. If they reject us, they just rejected Christ, because we are as Christ unto them (Luke 19:13).

When we received Jesus, we received the whole kingdom of God. The kingdom is in us, we are already saved; we are so saved, that we are in heaven (Colossians 3:3, I John 2:5). So we're not to worry anymore about going to heaven, there's a set time for that; now our job is to bring heaven to earth i.e. our homes, our place of work etc. It's time to shine God's light.

Own Comment

____
____
____
____
____
____
____
____
____

Prayer-

Dear Father, I thank You for bringing me into Your kingdom. I declare that the kingdom of God is within me and I am a light to this generation. My words and actions shall reflect the glory of the One who called me. Amen.

YOU ARE LOVED
DAY 7

To the praise of the glory of his grace, wherein he hath made us accepted in the beloved.
Ephesians 1:6

Many times, we are rejected before we are accepted. In some cases we enter into a place only to struggle to be noticed. And we sometimes cry to fit in or get accepted in a family and group that we are born to. We labour and strive against labels placed on us by people that we think should love us. Sometimes we pay to be loved and beg to be accepted. I know many of us have been overlooked in life making us feel insignificant and unwanted in affairs.

These are true emotions that run through us and we wonder, "does God feel the same way too?" I've got good news for you, you have been accepted in the beloved (Ephesians 1:6), you are accepted in a place where you don't have to work for it. Beloved, you are valuable to God, known by Him before you were formed, and set aside for an assignment before you came out of the womb. You and I have been uniquely designed for a function; and it doesn't matter who refuses to recognize and understand, it doesn't change the truth that you matter to God, and you are loved by Him.

Before I formed thee in the belly I knew thee; and before thou camest forth out of the womb I sanctified thee, and I ordained thee a prophet unto the nations.
Jeremiah 1:5

Beloved, it doesn't matter who dislikes you, you will be fine.

Other's Comment

Yvette Cameron
I find comfort in the fact that God sees and knows everything about us yet He loves us anyway. I read somewhere someone said, God is never disillusioned about you because He never had any illusions about you to begin with. Romans 8:38-39 tells us nothing in all creation shall be able to separate us from the love God has for us in Christ Jesus

Own Comment

____
____
____
____
____
____
____
____
____

Prayer

Dear Father, I thank You for knowing me, loving me and accepting me. I declare I am accepted in God's family and I am not an outcast. I shall not struggle to be noticed or accepted because I already matter where it matters. Amen.

BEWARE OF RELIGIOUS MINDSETS
DAY 8

All the ways of a man are clean in his own eyes; but the LORD weigheth the spirits.
Proverbs 16:2

With God, your motives give you away. Peter proclaimed love for Jesus, but was opposed to the will of God for His life (Matthew 16:21-23).
Saul offered sacrifice in total disobedience. (1 Samuel 13:8-9)

Religion can make you do things for God without a good heart; charity without Christ, praying with the wrong motives (James 4:3), Paul was persecuting Christ thinking he was doing God a service and the high priest rent his clothes calling Jesus a sinner.
Judas showed so much concern for the poor, yet was seeking to betray Christ (John 12:4-8).
Religion veils your heart from true repentance: having a form of godliness but denying the power thereof (2 Timothy 3:5).
Beloved, God weighs the spirit, He tries the heart and your motives are clear as glass before Him.
LOVE is the only motive that passes divine test. The kingdom of God is founded on the pillars of love. Service and offering in the kingdom stand on the foundation of love.
If any man love not the Lord, let him be Anathema Maranatha (1 Corinthians 16:22).
1 Corinthians 8:3 says, "if any man love God, the same is known of him."
Beloved, filter everything you say and do through the spectrum of love. If you grow in love daily, whatever you do and say will be accepted by God. Against love there is no law, or religion, or legality. (Galatians 5:22-23)
The bible says "we have passed from death to life because we love the brethren" (1 John 3:14) Amen.
Grow in love daily and you are doing fine.

Other's Comments

Shawnette James
This one definitely gives me something to ponder on.........Thanks

Angel David
.....so true. Religion kills, destroys lives and destinies. It is so incredibly frustrating being in religion and it also

hinders the plan of God. I am so glad my mind is renewed, now I can partake of God's grace

Own Comment

____

____

____

____

____

____

____

____

____

-

<u>Prayer</u>

Dear Father, I thank You for knowing me and putting Your love in my heart. I declare I am growing in love daily, my heart is pure and my motives are clear. My offerings and service shall all be done in love in Jesus name.

GET UP NOW
DAY 9

And Joshua said unto the children of Israel, How long are ye slack to go to possess the land, which the LORD God of your fathers hath given you? Joshua 18:3

Yes God has given the land, but to possess was left to them. The land was subdued before them and yet seven of the tribes were yet to possess the land and enter their inheritance.

In verse 1, they settled at Shiloh, and enjoyed the spiritual atmosphere; and not until Joshua woke them up they had no interest in the inheritance. They would rather go to church and go to heaven; this is the state of the church today. Joshua rebuked them for ***being slack, neglecting the inheritance***.

Many of us today don't like to be told what to do, or pushed, or prodded. We grew up in a system where we don't appreciate being chided or openly corrected. But most times, great leadership is about provoking people to rise to the challenge, so Joshua had to rebuke the people for slackness and negligence.

Beloved, there are many of us yet to possess our inheritance, the land is subdued before us but we settle down to enjoy the Shiloh experience. We need to get up now into the market place and take what belongs to us. It's time to intensify the prayer, increase in worship and anointing because we are in possession time. In Jesus name you shall not miss your own portion. Be not slack, get up in Jesus name.

Own Comment

____

____

____

Prayer

Dear Father, I thank You for opening my eyes to see all you have done for me and given to me in Christ Jesus. I declare I have a portion and I have an inheritance laid up for me. I shall not be slack in laying hold on my blessing, healing, favour, mercy, joy, riches and glory in Jesus name.

REFUSED TO BE CALLED BY THE OLD NAME
DAY 10

By faith Moses, when he was come to years, refused to be called the son of Pharaoh's daughter;

Hebrews 11:24

Our past most times are full of things and events we would not like to remember. Running from our past, some of us change names and location, seeking a fresh start, a new beginning.

Many of us run around looking for forgiveness from men, but one thing is sure; men can't give what they don't have. Men may forgive you sometimes, but you can be sure they will never forget it because your past is what they have as an advantage over you. In politics, in social circles and generally in life men seek to look into your past. And it may not matter where you run to, they will dig it out. But aren't you glad that God is not a man, and He has chosen to forget your past? (Isaiah 43:19).

For I will be merciful to their unrighteousness, and their sins and their iniquities will I remember no more.   Hebrews 8:12

But Moses was a little bit different though. He had a past that many of us would like to glory in; he was supposed to be a son of Pharaoh's daughter, the royal pride. But yet he chose to reject his past by refusing to be identified with it. He refused to be called a son of Pharaoh's daughter because of destiny.

Beloved, we have a better heritage, a better family and a better identity in Christ. You are the son of God, a seed of Abraham, a citizen of Zion and in the family of Christ on earth. As you embrace your new identity, only then can you be free from the past and the hold of men over you. Refuse to answer any name that men call you, because that is designed to put you under.

You are a new creature in Christ, old things are passed away (1 Corinthians 5:17) Your sins are no more and your past has no bearing with your future. It doesn't matter how many are looking at your past, as long as you refuse to look at it, God will do a new thing with you and for you. (Isa.43:19)

Beloved, embrace your new identity in Christ. It is a glorious destiny. Amen.

Own Comment

____

Prayer:

Dear Father, I thank You for giving me a new name and identity through Christ Jesus my Lord. I declare I am a seed of Abraham, a son of God, a member of Christ and a new creature. My sins are forgiven and my past is behind me therefore my future shall not be disrupted in Jesus name.

FREEDOM FROM LUST
DAY 11

"For I reckon that the sufferings of this present time are not worthy to be compared with the glory which shall be revealed in us. For the earnest expectation of the creature waiteth for the manifestation of the sons of God. For the creature was made subject to vanity, not willingly, but by reason of him who hath subjected the same in hope, Because the creature itself also shall be delivered from the bondage of corruption into the glorious liberty of the children of God. For we know that the whole creation groaneth and travaileth in pain together until now." Romans 8:18-22

The manifestation of the sons of God is to declare liberty and free the creation from the bondage of corruption. Beloved aren't you glad that you have escaped the corruption that is in this world through lust?

Whereby are given unto us exceeding great and precious promises: that by these ye might be partakers of the divine nature, having escaped the

corruption that is in the world through lust. 2Pet. 1:4

The world is decaying because of corruption. The bible clearly states that what makes up the world is lust. (1John2:15) This world eats, drinks and does business in lust. From the television to the internet, to schools to politics and sports, humanity is given to lust. Today's children are so corrupted with lust that they cannot differentiate between lust and love anymore.

Lust is the sickness of the flesh. It corrupts motives and judgement and blinds the eyes. Lust is selfish, seeks its own first and is eager to divide and separate. Lust reacts badly if it doesn't have its way. Lust seeks momentary pleasure, is never satisfied and can never be pleased in spite of consequences. Lust drives desires in pursuit of carnal and foolish things, will always manipulate, make more demands but slow to give.

Lust in the body of creation is the reason why men are so vulnerable to temptation because we are drawn by lust to commit sin. (James1:13-14).

Beloved aren't you glad you are free from the lust of this world which is the sin in the flesh? Your old man was crucified with Christ.

"Knowing this, that our old man is crucified with him, that the body of sin might be destroyed, that henceforth we should not serve sin." Rom. 6:6

"I am crucified with Christ: nevertheless I live; yet not I, but Christ liveth in me: and the life which I now live in the flesh I live by the faith of the Son of God, who loved me, and gave himself for me." ***Gal. 2:20***

"And they that are Christ's have crucified the flesh with the affections and lusts." ***Gal. 5:24***

The gospel of Jesus Christ thrives only on love. You will make a mess of it driven by the lust of fame, money and power.

"For the love of Christ constraineth us; because we thus judge, that if one died for all, then were all dead:" ***2Cor. 5:14***

Having escaped the corruption that is in the world through lust you cannot be entangled again with it. You cannot be a preacher of liberty while entangled with lust.

"While they promise them liberty, they themselves are the servants of corruption: for of whom a man is overcome, of the same is he brought in bondage.

For if after they have escaped the pollutions of the world through the knowledge of the Lord and Saviour Jesus Christ, they are again entangled therein, and overcome, the latter end is worse

with them than the beginning."

2Pet. 2:19-20

You are free from lust, you are not of this world. I believe we remain in this world to teach and share the kingdom principles and keys that the will of our Father may be done on earth

Own Comment

____
____
____
____
____
____
____
____
____

Prayer:

Dear Father, I thank You for freeing me from the bondage of corruption. I declare that my body of sin is destroyed through the dying of my Lord Jesus Christ on the tree. I shall no longer be subject to the dictates of my flesh and I shall not be ruled by lust in Jesus name.

DELIVERANCE FROM WORRYING
DAY 12

Therefore I say unto you, Take no thought for your life, what ye shall eat, or what ye shall drink; nor yet for your body, what ye shall put on. Is not the life more than meat, and the body than raiment?

Matthew 6:22

Worrying can be addictive, it can be a lifestyle and habitual. Many of us love to worry because of the sweetening effect and feelings we derive from the practice. While some of us just worry because that's the only thing we know how to do in response to every challenging situation.

The system we live in is designed to train us to worry about everything. The news we hear daily from media, friends and colleagues induce us to worry. We worry about our health; we need to go for check-ups with the doctor to make sure something is not growing unnoticed.

We worry about our jobs because there are no guarantees and security, we worry about our stock, we worry about our finances, we worry about our relationships, our children, future and the list is endless. So worrying has become a daily lifestyle that we have become used to, not knowing the repercussive effect of worrying.

We worry for one simple reason: **THERE IS NO GUARANTEE IN THIS LIFE.** We don't know what is coming tomorrow. Many of us are easily gripped with fear when we hear news like Japan's earthquake, sudden death of a close friend, a neighbor losing their job, our friends' relationship break up. So we assume if we can get a guarantee for our health, job, security etc. then we will stop worrying. Some of us tie our hopes on government, contract letters and some promises, and even then we still lack the assurance that things won't go wrong. And the more we see the end results of those who chose not to worry but resigned themselves to their "fate" and became laid back, the more we feel justified that man can't do without worrying.

But beloved, if you are in Christ, I have good news for you. Christ came to stop this worrying madness of yours. Only in Him do we have guarantee of anything. (2 Corinthians 2:10) If He can take care of the sparrows and the lilies of the valleys, you are certainly worth more than that before Him. Worrying is a choice, the bible says be careful for nothing. (Philippians 4:6) Worrying is an evidence of lack of faith and trust in the Almighty, and a lack of faith and trust in the love of God for you. Worrying will cut short the manifestation of His hand in your life. If you will stop worrying and start trusting, He will surely bring you out.

Other's Comments:

Sarissa Ryan

This is amazing, because I can truly relate to this message. It is true many people do typically lay back and worry because that is what the world expects from today's society. Worrying just weighs you down but if you are wise then you know how to avoid it, get stronger and move forward in your race to the finish line. No man is worth the worry.......

Angel David
Haha....I like that statement, "Christ came to stop this worrying madness of yours." So true....We worry about this and that and many times our day and time are so consumed with worry. We wake up worrying and go to bed worrying. And when you cannot handle the worry anymore, you become laid back, put on a, "don't have a care in the world attitude" which is another deception of the enemy.....it is total madness. And this is why I like this scripture, john 14:1, "Let not your heart be troubled: ye believe in God, believe also in me," It is time to believe God's word because whatsoever He said He would do, He will do it.

Own Comment

____
____
____
____
____
____
____
____
____

Prayer:

Dear Heavenly Father, thank You for being my guarantee in this life. In You all my needs are met according to Your riches in glory by Christ Jesus. I am the apple of Your eyes and You care for me as Your child. I refuse to worry or fret about any situation that may come my way in Jesus name.

MOUNTAIN VALLEY MOUNTAIN I
DAY13

Then answered Peter, and said unto Jesus, Lord, it is good for us to be here: if thou wilt, let us make here three tabernacles; one for thee, and one for Moses, and one for Elias.
Matthew 17:4

The story of Israel and their journey to the promised land is a reflective picture of our spiritual journey today in Christ. On the seventh day the Lord selected just three of the disciples, Peter, James and John to witness the glory of His transformation on the mountain. And two special guests; Elijah and Moses joined them in the spectacle.

It was a superb experience for Peter; the peace, the joy, the harmony he felt in the glory of His presence prompted him to make a grand request "...Lord please don't let us go down, let us stay here with you, it doesn't matter if we have no tabernacle to ourselves; we will stay with You, Moses and Elijah." How could Peter have so soon forgotten his colleagues and family below. The mountain experience is so joyous and glorious, many of us today feel the same ecstasy and the joy of His presence, under the canopy of His glory; it's an amazing feeling.

But quite expectedly, Jesus did not grant Peter`s request. His prayer request was turned down because they had to leave the mountain (Matthew 17:9). It was a momentary experience designed for a purpose, for they had work to do down in the valley. From Matthew 17:14-19 they were contending with demons in others' lives and paying taxes. The valley experience is not what many of us envisage and love but that is where the fruit of the spirit and divine character is groomed. Nobody harvests fruits on the mountain, it's done in the valley.

Other's Comment

Precious London

This was a message of deliverance for me. I had continuously been striving to stay on the mountain, and I believe that is where we are actually designed to live and dwell on a day to day basis... in private times with the Lord. In continuously seeking to dwell on the mountain like Peter, we can subconsciously begin to despise the valley, opening the door to shame, bitterness and mostly

condemnation. This message came and brought clarification to the truth that when you are in Him, there are blessings to be attained both on the mountain and in the valley. One is not to be despised over the other, but both are for the edification of your spirit and ultimately to bring glory to His name.
James 1:1-4

Own Comment

____
____
____
____
____
____
____
____
____

-

Prayer:

Thank You Father because you are the God of the mountain and also of the valley. Your love for me is constant, I refuse to look back in the valley and on the mountain You will always be my God. I receive strength to rejoice in You always.

MOUNTAIN VALLEY MOUNTAIN II
DAY14

The valley is a place of trial and test of our faith. This is where we're made, prepared, and used by God. It's a place where we build strength, virtue and wisdom; a place where we learn to place absolute trust in the Lord.

The enemy has always challenged God and our ability to stand in the valley. He snobs your mountain experience and says, "...see you in the valley..." Satan snubbed at Job's faithfulness and integrity. "..... Is it not because he is on the mountain with you.... business is good and life is great.... let me try him out at the valley and he will curse you to your face...." (Job 1:9-10)

How could the devil be so sure that Job would curse God. He seems to know the sons of men very well...that in the valley most people won't trust the Lord or they fail in faith. The devil may have criss-crossed all countries and claim to know sons of men but he was wrong about Job.

God is ever determined to shut the enemies up, so God is also saying "...okay, let us go to the valley".

And there came a man of God, and spake unto the king of Israel, and said, Thus saith the LORD, Because the Syrians have said, The LORD is God of

the hills, but he is not God of the valleys, therefore will I deliver all this great multitude into thine hand, and ye shall know that I am the LORD.

1 King 20:28

The enemies of your life are shut down permanently in the valley days of your life so you can be qualified for the second mountain experience which is permanent, is a realm of rest and glory, a rehoboth, a season when the enemies gives up and leave you alone(Luke 4:13, Gen.26:22). KEEP HOLDING ON TO FAITH AND TRUST IN GOD and Your glory days are here. Amen.

Own Comment

____
____
____
____
____
____
____
____
____

Prayer:

Father thank You for your love for me always. The trial of my faith is precious in Your sight even much more than gold. I am a person of integrity, I receive grace and mercy to stand strong in whatever test or trial of faith I am going through.

MOUNTAIN VALLEY MOUNTAIN III
DAY 15

Joseph had a great youth life; he had favour with his father, was given a coat of many colours and then capped with a fantastic dream of a great destiny and future. Little did he know that the path to that destiny was through the prison and the pit. God prepared him by teaching him to interpret others' dreams while his own dream was in the cooler.

He had to experience hatred, envy, rejection and be forgotten by those he helped. I'm very sure in his life he got to a point he asked, "Oh Lord, why have you forsaken me?" The Lord Jesus had to descend before His ascension. He had to fight below before His final glorification.

(Now that he ascended, what is it but that he also descended first into the lower parts of the earth?

He that descended is the same also that ascended up far above all heavens, that he might fill all things.)

Ephesians 4:9-10

Beloved, after your valley experience is coming the second mountain experience. These are the days of your glorification. You may have been going through the wilderness, desert or valley life, you are only being prepared for the days of glory. Our first mountain experience as we come to know the Lord is "taste and see the Lord is good". And we suddenly plummet to the valley to be made and strengthened, and then He brings us out back to the mountain which is a reward of His glory.

Other's Comments

Yvette Cameron

I like what you said, "after your valley experience is coming your second mountain experience", which means if you are in a valley look up. When you are down there is no place to go but up. The challenge is to keep the faith and expectation until your change comes. In his valley experience Job said, "All the days of my struggle I will wait UNTIL my change comes" and it did. He was rewarded double for his trouble.

Own Comment

____
____
____
____
____
____
____
____
____

Prayer:

Thank You Father, for the spirit of glory that rests upon me. You have brought me out to set me up on the Rock to stand and praise Your name. I am living for Your glory and Your goodness in the name of Jesus.

MOUNTAIN VALLEY MOUNTAIN IV
DAY 16

Beloved, it is all about how well you do in the valley; if you will not be bitter you will surely get better (Genesis 50:20). David began from the palace, then to the wilderness. But in the days of his exile he excelled in character (Psalm 35:11-15), and he learned to trust in the presence of the Almighty alone.

Yea, though I walk through the valley of the shadow of death, I will fear no evil: for thou art with me; thy rod and thy staff they comfort me.

Psalm 23:4

Beloved are there areas in your life you are yet to put absolute trust in the Lord? Those are the areas where God will have to take you to the valley. Some of us can trust God in everything but our finances, or our health, or children, or for God to provide a partner, or keep our relationship. So everyday we`re tempted to resolve to carnal and fleshy means. Beloved you are on the way to the valley where we all learn to put absolute trust in the Lord and everything He has promised. Apostle Paul says we have a sentence of death in ourselves and have learnt not to put trust in ourselves.

But we had the sentence of death in ourselves, that we should not trust in ourselves, but in God which raiseth the dead:

2 Corinthians 1:9

Beyond your valley experience is coming the days of glory. I rejoice with you, be strong and never give up.

Own Comment

____
____
____
____
____
____
____
____
____

Prayer:

Thank You Father because of Your faithfulness to Your word. You will never leave me or forsake me. You are with me right now through all my struggles. I have Your Holy Spirit in me and upon me. Father I obtain mercy and grace never to give up until I show forth Your goodness and greatness to this generation.

KISSES OF ENEMIES
DAY 17

Faithful are the wounds of a friend; but the kisses of an enemy are deceitful. ***Prov. 27:6***

Wherefore putting away lying, speak every man truth with his neighbour: for we are members one of another. ***Eph. 4:25***

There are very few of us who really don't like kisses, but some of the time we don`t know who is kissing us. The Lord is our strength but often times use genuine friends to expose our weaknesses to us. You can confess your fault to a genuine friend and you can be sure he/she is praying for you and with you. (James 5:16)

A mentor or God-given friend is never afraid to tell you your fault or expose your weakness to you and will be strong to stand by you in your fight to overcome it. Such a friend will also not hesitate to cut you off if you are not doing anything about it. (2Thes. 3:6, 1Cor. 5:2,5)

Friendship and mentoring in the kingdom is more about helping of destinies, sharpening of strength and strengthening of weaknesses more than social companionship or filling the emotional void of loneliness. (Prov. 27:17)

On the other hand evil friends may discover your weakness and faults and never tell you to your face but have no qualms exposing you to the world or gossiping about you at the dining table and then abandon you to deal with the consequences. That is not the kind of friend you want kissing you. You don't need an enemy with a friend like that.

Jesus never excused weaknesses and unbelief in the disciples. They were rebuked instantly. Apostle Paul encouraged godly sorrow in the Corinthian church, refusing to give relief in their godly remorse. (2Cor. 7:8-11)

As believers we provide comfort during grief but refuse to ease discomfort during repentance. As genuine friends we refuse to look the other way. Exploiting, abusing and using other people`s weaknesses for your personal comfort is what makes you an enemy. Stop taking money you don't need, stop having sex with him or her simply because they are weak and you know you have no plans for them, stop using his or her credit card because they can`t say no and you know they don't have the income to repay. An enemy is the one that flatters you in your weakness. The bible says he is spreading a net for your feet. (Prov. 29:5)

Beloved stop seeking the praise of men, you might end up getting the wrong kiss. True and genuine friends are in Christ. There are those who will not polish the truth or embellish the story to make you feel good. (Ezek. 33:26, Col. 3:9)

Dear friend, do you really care about your friends in the world? You will be a good friend telling them about the consequences of rejecting the love of God which is Christ Jesus the Lord.

He that believeth on him is not condemned: but he that believeth not is condemned already, because he hath not believed in the name of the only begotten Son of God.

And this is the condemnation, that light is come into the world, and men loved darkness rather than light, because their deeds were evil. John 3:18-19

Other's Comments

Allison Khan

To appreciate the grace of God in your life is to appreciate Him for those whom He has placed in your life. Many of us go through life trying to be accepted for who we are and praised for what we do, that all of our energy is spent hiding our faults and weaknesses. God is in the business of building character and strength to carry you to your destiny in him. It is oftentimes those in your life who see those weaknesses and faults that God uses to do the building. We may not like who He chose or how He does it but we will definitely like the results. Our ability to recognize those God-given people will give speed to the course of fulfilling destiny.

Tremain Nembhard

One thing pastor Olu has said before is that "sheep give birth to sheep"
The bible says that help/strength comes from Zion.
God created the body, the church for a reason. No one is an island. There is wealth in relationships so a man minus relationships is a poor man.
With that being said anyone who is seeking to isolate themselves is seeking to hide their weaknesses, setting themselves up for destruction and are easy prey for the devil. God has placed certain people in your life to not only expose but help you to strengthen your weaknesses bringing to fruit godly character that is essential for your calling. Any excuse to remain isolated and the refusal to open to the help of a friend is a lie from the enemy.

Precious London

Wow! What a powerful message. You can guarantee that if you are one who looks for the praises of men, the enemy will be sure to lure you in with praises that will feed your ego and ruin your destiny. Christ was confident in His purpose and position. When the devil took Jesus onto the high mountain and promised Him the Kingdoms and their glory in exchange for worship, Jesus' response was, "...you shall worship the Lord your God, and Him only you shall serve." (Matthew 4:10). Then the devil left Him. Jesus was not tempted by the praises of men. He recognized that seeking worship from men would make Him a thief; stealing worship from God Almighty.

Knowing our position, calling and destiny in Christ will keep us free from being flattered and deceived by the kisses of an enemy, and appreciative of the faithful wounds of a friend.

Own Comment

____

Prayer:

Thank You Father for You have chosen for me a friend that sticks closer than a brother in Christ Jesus my Lord. You have also surrounded me with friends in my brothers and sisters in Christ. My mind and heart are open toYour instructions and corrections. I receive grace to receive truth in love. Chastise me with Your gentle love and I will be healed.

YOUR WORTH
DAY 18

Are not five sparrows sold for two farthings, and not one of them is forgotten before God?
But even the very hairs of your head are all numbered. Fear not therefore: ye are of more value than many sparrows.
Luke 12:6-7

Don't ever be surprised at the treatment you receive from people around you. Most times it is determined by their estimation of you. Estimate determines value and value determines treatment. Are you still angry at the government for looking out for the mineral resources, the economy of the land, for animals and the planet than they care about how you live your life? They have a country to run and elections to win.
Friends and neighbors will always estimate you and then put you in a box based on your past, your gift and talent, your bank balance, looks, position in life, job titles, your performance and achievements. Please don't get offended, they have to watch out for their own interest. That is the spirit of the world. The kingdom of men is governed by me, mine and I.

Sometimes our so called friends, family, children and even parents may forget to return our calls, invite us, forget our birthdays, omit our input etc, please don't lay it to their charge. They are not different from the sons of men.

But beloved aren't you glad that in the kingdom of God we derive our worth from God Himself? God`s estimate of you is very great (Is 43:4). To God the value of your soul is worth more than this world put together. (Mark 8:36). God treats you as though you are the only one on earth. The bible is written with you in mind. If you were the only one on this earth, He would have still come to die for your soul. The price on you is the price of Christ`s blood. Your worth is intrinsic and personal in nature, unique and incomparable to the things of this world.

Beloved aren't you glad that your position, your material stuff, your looks, your relationships, materials or whatsoever this world has to offer does not define you? Can you imagine the confidence and strength you will feel when you begin to see yourself the way God sees you? You are simply worth more than jewelry, sparrows, dogs etc. What God saw in you, that made him send His only begotten Son to shed His blood to buy you back from sin and death, is still in you today and right now. Aren't you glad that no matter who you are, where you are, what you are going through, what you have and don't have, what you have done or not done, your worth does not diminish, your value is still the same with God. You can rise today and call him Father. When you did not know Him, He died for you. When you were still a sinner, He cared. His love is constant because your worth is constant.

Beloved if you will recover your self- worth in Christ, you will soon begin to find your place in this world. Amen.

Other's Comments

Allison Khan-

Because many people in our lives are nice one day, mean tomorrow, loving today and hating tomorrow it's easy to think that God is that way too. We may think that God's opinion of us must be the same as everyone else's. After all, how could that many people be wrong? But that is not the case. 1Chron 17:17 David said "...and you have regarded me according to a man of high degree, O Lord God." You can only be confident in how God thinks of you if you know what He has said about you; and the Word of God tells you. Stop listening to those around you and find out the truth-what God says about you.

Sarissa Ryan

Amen. The price that God paid for me is worth so much more than any man can afford.

Yvette Cameron-

I am certainly glad that as was mentioned, position, material stuff, looks, relationships, materials or whatsoever this world has to offer does not define me. But I must say it took a mind renewal after coming into the kingdom to embrace this kind of thinking. But what a relief it is from the burden of measuring one's self worth by worldly standards. Thank God for the rest that is found in Christ and His estimation of us.

Own Comment

____

____

____

____

____
____
____
____
____

Prayer: Thank You Father for who You are. Your thoughts and estimation of me has never ceased to surprise me. I am beloved, favoured and precious in Your sight. I am confident in Your worth of me and I receive strength to maintain my worth in You. I refuse to look down on myself in Jesus name.

OBEDIENCE PAYS
DAY 19

Oh that my people had hearkened unto me, and Israel had walked in my ways! I should soon have subdued their my hand against their adversaries. The enemies, and turned haters of the LORD should have submitted themselves unto him: but their time should have endured for ever. He should have fed them also with the finest of the wheat: and with honey out of the rock should I have satisfied thee.
Psalm 81:13-16

The entire verses above can simply be summarized as, 'if they had listened and obeyed'. Many of us at one time or the other in our lives can relate to the above phrase and have said to ourselves, "if only I had listened and obeyed". It is amazing that we are not the only ones who show signs of regrets of our failure, God Himself in His love shows signs of regrets when we fail because He

doesn't want us to fail. You probably wonder why many of us still find it hard to listen and obey.
Beloved it is not too late to start listening, hearing and obeying. The sorrow of disobedience far outweighs the pains of obedience. You may never know what you have missed or are missing living a disobedient lifestyle until it is too late. Can you imagine what Israel missed?

1. The enemy should have been subdued. Is it not better to face a subdued enemy than to face a raging one? Many of us are still fighting battles that should have long been over. It is a complete waste of time fighting a battle that Christ has already won. Obedience is the key.
2. The adversary should have been contending with God's hand instead of with theirs. Life can be stress free if only we stay out of the battle zone and pitch behind God giving Him praise.
3. Haters of God should have submitted to them. This world is producing haters of God daily, all over the internet/media, waiting to submit to us if only we will listen and obey His voice. His manifestation of His glory and power will soon keep them quiet.
4. How could they have missed fine wheat and honey from the rock? The forces of prosperity are dictated by the condition of the heavens and earth. God is in charge of our economic system.

Abraham obeyed His voice and he was so blessed. (Gen. 22:17) Isaac was charged and reminded that the key to Abraham's blessing was his obedience to His voice. (Gen. 26:4-5) The Lord God rejected religious offering and demanded that Israel obey His voice, while stating that disobedience is the reason why they went backward and not forward. (Jer. 7:22-24)
Beloved, I see you moving forward in your life and destiny as you dedicate yourself to first class obedience

to His voice. Obeying His voice is the primary key of releasing Abraham's blessing over the work of your hands and possessing the good of the land. (Job 36:11, Isa. 1:19)

Comments

Yvette Cameron

I have really been meditating on this particular issue of obedience as it relates to the releasing of the Abrahamic blessing and I found something very interesting. God called Abram out said He would bless him in Gen 12:1-3 and He was blessed but in Gen 22:16 -17. God came again at the ALTAR OF SACRIFICE and gave Abraham a SWORN BLESSING. My question is: Why did God do that? Wasn't Abraham already blessed?

Sarissa Ryan

It has taken me many years to really listen and obey what I have been told but now I am getting better and growing higher day by day

Allison Khan

I wonder why it's hard for us at times to obey God. Do we think He's wrong? Do we think we know better? Do we think He's just trying to make our life difficult? The truth is that our blessing is tied to our obedience. The whole 28th chapter of Deuteronomy compares the pros of obeying the commandments and the curses of disobeying. Isaiah 1:19 says only those who are willing and obedient will eat the good of the land. Job 36:11 tells us that those who obey and serve the Lord will spend their lifetime in pleasure and prosperity. So not only does obeying the voice and instructions of the Lord keep us in partnership with Him but also brings peace and blessing to us.

Angel David

Philippians 2:8-9: "And being found in fashion as a man, he humbled himself, and became obedient unto death, even the death of the cross. Wherefore God also hath highly exalted him, and given him a name which is above every name."
Jesus was obedient to carry out the will of God to the end, word by word, letter by letter; and then God exalted Him and gave Him a name above all names as a result of His obedience. It is the same way now, when we obey God completely and whole heartedly then we have our reward.

Leshar Shaw

Since I started to target my weaknesses God has really been showing me a lot about obedience. The only way you can even be obedient is by hearing, then listening and then you obey (hear, listen, obey). One enemy of obedience is a hearing problem. If you don't hear the instructions properly you won't obey correctly.
I was doing a study on the heart and I found that obedience is a heart issue. King Amaziah did the right thing in the sight of the Lord but not with a perfect heart (1 Chron. 25:2), and because he didn't have a perfect heart he also couldn't hear (1 Chron. 25:20). King Saul couldn't obey a simple instruction which was to wait. The Lord replaced Saul with a man after his own heart (1 Sam 12:14). Obedience is saying Lord my heart is yours, my will, my plan, my desire etc. When your heart is after God's heart obedience will come naturally.

Own Comment

Prayer: Father, thank You because You are always speaking to me. My ears are open. You have my undivided attention. I obtain mercy and grace to always listen, hear and obey Your voice in Jesus name.

LESSON OF CONTENTMENT
DAY 20

Not that I speak in respect of want: for I have learned, in whatsoever state I am, therewith to be content. ***Phil. 4:11***

Paul had to learn the godly lesson of contentment. I wonder when many of us will learn that the gain of godliness is the contentment therewith.

But godliness with contentment is great gain.
1Tim.6:6

Discontentment is a disease of the soul plaguing humanity. Have you not noticed that everywhere you go to, all over the land, the voices of dissatisfaction, grumbling, complaining and the aroma of discontent fills the air?

Can you imagine people eating bread (manna) baked by God and yet were fed up? (Num 6:4-10)

"But now our soul is dried away: there is nothing at all, beside this manna, before our eyes. ....Then Moses heard the people weep throughout their families, every man in the door of his tent: and the anger of the LORD was kindled greatly; Moses also was displeased." Num.11:6,10

Does it not cease to amaze you how many claim to have Jesus today and are still not satisfied? It has to be Jesus plus something. And often time if that thing doesn't come, grumbling and discontentment begins. How about the man that God blessed with a beautiful wife at home but cannot just stop looking out until he commits adultery. The political system today is saturated with unrest; protest of millions of voices of discontent. Someone will ride on their discontent, make promises, win the election, only to be voted out again by the angry mob. Why? Because there is nothing out there besides the Living Christ that can satisfy the hungry soul.
In discontentment, people cry and crave for new stuff and new style at all times. The business and marketing world are making a fortune recycling and changing designs of products to make them look new so they can feed this desire and longing for something new. It was plasma TV, now it is LED, tomorrow we will have 'LOD'. It was ipod now we have ipad, soon we will have 'ipeg'. The crave for new things is not the same as improved lifestyle or better living condition. Of course God will

always give us something better, if we are grateful for what we have and use them to the fullest.
Discontentment stems from lust and it breeds comparison, complain and grumbling which makes you very vulnerable. Driven by lust, discontent makes a wanderer out of many believers. Drawn by need, many have left the place that God put them and are trapped in error.
Beloved, you are complete in Him. You have drunk of the living water. You are satisfied in /with Christ. Your search is over. You are blessed in Him. Jesus Christ is all you need and have ever wanted.

Other's Comments

Aileen Galve- Amen, we need to be thankful for every little thing God has given us and for everything He has done for us. You definitely don't want to be a complainer sowing seeds of discontent, you'll never be happy with anything

Sarissa Ryan

I agree with this because I have gone through this. At first I wanted Christ and a boyfriend, but now I'm content with where I am.

Lizzy Brown

Amen, I really enjoyed reading this.

Own Comment

____

____

____

____

____

____

____

____

____

Prayer:

Dear Father, thank You because You are my Sufficiency, my El-Shaddai in everything. I am satisfied with what You have given me. I refuse to covet, complain or grumble. In the name of Jesus I receive strength to be stable where You have placed me.

THE WAR IS OVER

DAY 21

Comfort ye, comfort ye my people, saith your God.

Speak ye comfortably to Jerusalem, and cry unto her, that her warfare is accomplished, that her iniquity is pardoned: for she hath received of the LORD's hand double for all her sins. Isa. 40:1-2

Sometimes looking around you, your experiences, your life struggles coupled with the challenges that we face daily and those that lie ahead of us, we are programed to think that this life is full of warfare and there are battles all around.

With this kind of mindset, we approach life with a warfare attitude. And sometimes we fight through everything and everybody that comes our way.

We are born to trust but we grow learning how to distrust. We are born to love but grow up learning to hate. We learn so many things on the way, acquire so many negative weapons, all in our quest to win.

At the end of the day, like most celebrities in life and in Hollywood especially, we end up with pains, frustrations, regrets, wounds, dissatisfaction and along the way we breed more enemies to fight tomorrow.

When will the war be over? In our soul, in our body, with our health, our image and the list is endless.

Beloved, I have great news for you, if you can believe. Your warfare is accomplished, your sins are forgiven. The Lion of the tribe of Judah has prevailed. Jesus Christ has won the battle. He spoilt the enemies beyond recovery.

And having spoiled principalities and powers, he made a shew of them openly, triumphing over them in it. Col. 2:15

Beloved, do you want to know why many of us fight the battle that Christ has already won?

1. Religious mindset- Religion tells you that you have to do something of yourself. It is more about what you can do than what Christ did. In Christ, faith and liberty is comprehending and declaring what the Lord has done. Yes we have to do something; we live by faith by declaring the victory of Christ. (1Cor. 15:57)
2. Unhealthy fear of the enemy- Only in the mind of an unregenerated soul is the devil the opposite of God, a form of God or can do what God can do. There is nothing farther from the truth than that. The devil is a loser and does not deserve your fear or worship. He lost the battle in heaven, at Calvary and in the depth of the earth. He is a prisoner of war, stripped and naked, a condemned criminal waiting for execution. There is only one God and He is the Lord of all. God has no opposite. He alone dwells in and inhabits eternity. There are no two Creators. Jesus Christ alone is the One.

Beloved you are in Christ and in Christ you have no more war to fight. The enemy is subdued. Your business is to

declare Christ's victory daily by casting him out of where he shouldn't be, resisting him from coming into a place he shouldn't be and commanding him in authority. (James 4:7, 1Pet. 5:9 and Mark 16:17)
What do you think of someone you can freely command, cast out and resist? This is the way you should think about your struggles, opposition and what you face daily. Keep on winning in Jesus' name.

Other's Comments

Aileen Galve
The battle was finished a long time ago, Jesus Christ has already won. We are in Christ therefore we have the victory. The devil is a loser and a liar. The only thing he can do is try to make you believe he has power. God has given us authority over the devil and his demons (Luke 10:19). Praise the Lord, we are victorious!

Own Comment

____
____
____
____
____
____
____
____
____

Prayer:
Thank You heavenly Father for the breakthrough You have given me in Christ Jesus. I am a winner in this life and in the name of Jesus I claim victory over sickness, poverty and sin. I declare victory over depression, shame and guilt in Jesus name.

WHY SHOULD HE CARE
DAY 22

Though the LORD be high, yet hath he respect unto the lowly: but the proud he knoweth afar off. ***Psa. 138:6***

Why should God care about you and me, is a big question that comes to mind when you sit back to consider His awesomeness, His greatness and the splendour of His majesty through the works of His hands and where He dwells. Much more so when you know that in light of the world we live in and our day to day experiences, it is not common to see the so called big guys, the successful people, the high and the lofty of the land, the mighty people or rich people express a desire to associate with others they think are lowly placed.

David was simply stunned at this amazing strength when he thought of God being mindful of you and me in spite of His greatness and awesomeness.
When I consider thy heavens, the work of thy fingers, the moon and the stars, which thou hast ordained; What is man, that thou art mindful of

him? and the son of man, that thou visitest him? Psa. 8:3-4

In our world, it is often an aberration to see the 'highly placed and classed' wanting to associate with the lowly. Everybody wants to be a friend of the successful. The Prime minister may tell you how much he loves and cares for you but be sure he won't be dining with you at the mall. The rich man may tell you, you are valuable but he may discourage his daughter from marrying you. Every day the ex-convicts are told that they are human beings and that they still matter, but may still find it difficult to get a second chance or a job.

In this world of ours associating with the lowly is not common place. Unfortunately this also happens in our churches. You will not look too far to find people associating with big time churches and pastors because that is just the nature of men. But it is not so in the kingdom. Having accepted Jesus, you and I like Moses have chosen to be with the people of God in their low estate.(Heb.11:25)

Beloved aren't you glad that God is not a man? He cares about the lowly. He is mindful of you and me. He resists the proud and gives grace to the humble. (1Pet. 5:6) He opens His treasures and secrets to babes.(Luke 10:21) He has ordained strength in the mouth of children. (Psa. 8:2) He will rather choose to manifest himself in a still and small voice. (1Kgs. 19:12)

Isn't it wonderful to know that when/where men cannot sit with you, where they cannot go with you and the walk they don't want to walk with you, that Christ is eager to be with you all the way and be your friend? He can do all this because of His LOVE and STRENGTH. He alone deserves your praise and appreciation.

Other's Comments

Precious London

It is the Adamic nature in man that propels him to leave the "lowly" in order to be found among the rich and prosperous...even in the church. But if we are truly in Christ and are born of His spirit, then we will find ourselves drawn to those in need; the widows, the fatherless, the abused, the abandoned and the poor. Thank God that Christ, in His passion and compassion, came and died so that we could have life and have it more abundantly. In Him, the poor are made rich and the weak strong. His love for us has made a way well beyond material possessions. Thank God for His love!

Allison Khan

This is amazing. The One who placed the stars in the heaven, who paints the sky to display His glory is thinking about me? Concerned about me? Loving me? To think that the smallest of our problems we magnify so much that it actually blocks the view of this Mighty and Majestic God. We are not small in His eyes. Thank You Jesus.

David Foster

Although He is High yet he wants to fellowship with the humble. He cares about us but it is time spent in His presence, the experience of Him filling your atmosphere with His glory that helps to see His greatness and His great love towards us. He is High yet those who think themselves high (the proud) are the ones He is far away from. What a mystery our God is!

Yvette Cameron

I really thank God for the hope that is found in Christ. To know that He cares all the time is a secure anchor for the soul against the hopelessness that may try to invade our lives at times when we are disappointed by people. He is our Abba Father (Rom 8:15) , He is Jehovah Nissi - The Lord our Banner (Ex 17:15) and His banner over us is LOVE (Song of Sol 2:4).

Own Comment:

____
____
____
____
____
____
____
____
____

Prayer:

Father, thank You for Your strength and Your gentleness. You are a Mighty God but You chose to dwell in me. Your thoughts of me are great. I am grateful I am Your son. In the name of Jesus Christ every tongue of condemnation against me is silenced forever. I am seated with Christ in the heavenly places.

STRENGTH TO WAIT FOR HIM
DAY 23

My flesh and my heart faileth: but God is the strength of my heart, and my portion for ever.
Psa. 73:26

Receiving the word and the promises of God is actually a lesser task then waiting for the manifestation of them. The challenging thing about God's words, promises and visions is that sometimes they 'tarry'.

For the vision is yet for an appointed time, but at the end it shall speak, and not lie: though it tarry, wait for it; because it will surely come, it will not tarry. Habk. 2:3

Why should any man wait for twenty -five years to have a child? Abraham did! (Gen 12:4,7; 21:5) David was anointed to be king at 16 in his father's house, his coronation never took place until he was thirty. Only God knows when Jesus is returning. The Son of God is still waiting on His Father. It must have taken Job more than mere determination to wait out his trouble.

If a man die, shall he live again? all the days of my appointed time will I wait, till my change come. Job 14:14

These great men knew that God's promises, manifestations and visions are worth waiting for.

It is good that a man should both hope and quietly wait for the salvation of the LORD. Lam. 3:26

Beloved, are there promises, manifestations and words you are waiting for in your life and it looks like it is taking forever?

Yes, I know. Sometimes it could be heart weakening especially when you suddenly find yourself under pressure to perform in a fast paced world and facing reproaches around you.

You will probably wonder what does it take to wait for God. Why should I wait for long? How did Abraham, David, Job and others do it?
Beloved the answer is in **waiting on Him**. ***We wait on Him so that we can wait for Him***. We wait on Him to receive strength in our heart.

Wait on the LORD: be of good courage, and he shall strengthen thine heart: wait, I say, on the LORD. Psa. 27:14

We wait on Him by staying in His presence to worship and adore and then we are equipped with strength in our hearts to wait for Him. Ask a server/waitress. They wait on their guests probably for better tips. But we do wait on the Lord for strength to wait for His promise. You can never overvalue the excellence of the character and patience you develop in the process. You will be perfect and entire wanting nothing. (James 1:4)

Other's Comments

Angel David-The game of waiting is never an easy one especially since we live in a fast paced world and everything being convenient. You can have dinner in 5mins just pop it into the microwave. We have drive-thrus so you don't need to get out of your car, drugs to help you lose weight and so on. So we don't have to struggle to get most things; but with God it is a whole different game, patience is key to seeing the blessing manifest. That was the one thing I didn't like but God needs us to be patient, to keep remembering. And to have patience you need strength because if not you will forget and go back. Another thing is that God has been teaching me about praising and worshipping Him in songs and in words; that gives you supernatural strength. And in the midst of such beautiful worship, His presence is there and then He brings to remembrance the promises.

Also I love God. Before I came to this note, I was tired and then I saw that scripture Psalms 73:26 and I remembered a time in my life that I needed strength and God instantly healed my heart. I love that God is always covering me.

Precious London

The way we wait on Him determines the quality of waiting. As we wait on Him, it is crucial for us to remain in Him. All other waiting is done in vain and forces us to rely on our own fleshly strength to endure the wait. As a result, the prize cannot be received fully by us because we are lacking in the character to maintain it. In waiting, God builds in us the foundation necessary to maintain the blessing.

Own Comment

____
____
____
____
____
____
____
____
____

Prayer:

Dear heavenly Father, thank You for Your word and promises over me. I am a child of promise. I hold on to Your word. I am walking in divine blessings. I receive grace and strength to speak and stand on the word until they become flesh in Jesus name. Amen.

DESTINY IS WAITING FOR YOU
DAY 24

........:I being in the way, the LORD led me.......... Gen.24:27

Has it not ceased to amaze you how people come by destiny going about their assignment? Rebekah was at the well to draw water but destiny met her.

David was asked to go give lunch to his brothers at the battle field, destiny was waiting for him. (1Sam. 17:26-30) Saul was looking for his father's lost donkeys when destiny came calling. (1Sam. 9:3,20) Is it not amazing how these young men and women in helping out their parents came by divine destiny?

Beloved are you looking for destiny? It is right within your daily affairs. Be strong to help your parents, help your pastors in churches, help your neighbours and go about your daily business.

Something great is waiting for you out there.

Other's Comments

Angel David- WOW...my new favorite scripture Gen 24:27 " I being in the way, the Lord led me..." so true. All these men and women were not out there looking for destiny. It came to them while doing their service. I am amazed because God read my heart and answered my question AGAIN

Precious London- The word that has REALLY been resonating in my spirit over the past few months, is that blessing is found in obedience. My life has changed so much since I have been obedient in what I have committed to do. I am learning that blessings and treasures can be hidden in the crevices of your assignment. It is not to be taken lightly and we are not to fall complacent in the redundancy of routine. For we serve a God whose mercy is new every morning (Lamentations 3:23).

Allison Khan - This is so crucial. Many of us in wanting to know what we should do neglect what we should be doing. You will not be trusted with a larger assignment until you have been faithful in what you see as a small assignment. Joseph was called to interpret Pharaoh's dream because he had done well with the baker and the butler and given God the glory and this landed him in the palace

Amanda Foster- Being consistent in your obligations is so important. What if Rebekah woke up that morning, let the flesh prevail and she said " I'm not going, this is boring what's the point"? If that attitude prevailed, she would have missed destiny. Even if it seems tedious, or repetitive, it's in that you develop character, so by the time destiny comes calling, they will find a character fit to hold the call. This will definitely come from doing the things God asks you to do even when it seems small. Don't despise small beginings, it is the foundation of greatness

Azhia Julien- The one time Saul was obedient he found his destiny and also lost it through disobedience...Powerful. I like this message a lot. When you are faithful with the instructions from your parents/authority on earth, God will find you faithful to carry out His instructions. Hhmm.

Own Comments:

____
____
____
____
____
____
____
____
____

Prayer:

Father thank You so much for what You have in store and Your plan for my life. I have a glorious destiny in Christ. I refuse to give up. Lord I receive mercy and grace to do my daily schedules and assignments without complaint. Destiny is waiting for me. Amen.

AVOID DISTRACTION
DAY 25

And Eliab his eldest brother heard when he spake unto the men; and Eliab's anger was kindled against David, and he said, Why camest thou down hither? and with whom hast thou left those few sheep in the wilderness? I know thy pride, and the naughtiness of thine heart; for thou art come down that thou mightest see the battle.
And David said, What have I now done? Is there not a cause?
And he turned from him toward another,.............
1Sam. 17:28-30

Distraction has always been a very subtle tool of the enemy to steal our focus or to side track us from paying attention to the main thing.

Many homes are in jeopardy because the husband and the wife fight over small things. It has always taken little foxes to spoil the vine. Churches are divided daily over trivial issues while the kingdom assignment and vision lags terribly. If only believers will know what to overlook and avoid on their path to destiny. Sometimes what you have to do is just let go, so you can move on.

David has just come by an opportunity to fulfil divine destiny. He has just been motivated by an excellent reward. He is seeing a vision and the task ahead of him. Can you imagine who would have stopped him? It was his own brother who came down angrily on him and said, "......you have no business here........your motive is not right............you are too small for the task here........you belong somewhere else......"

Don't be surprised if people around you put you down because they are focusing on your limitations, but David would not be deterred. And because he understood the purpose he turned away from his brother.

Beloved you need to differentiate a brother from the enemy. Love will always win, is never easily offended, not issue-prone, it easily let go and cannot be tied down. Many times in life we react and respond to things that we should just let go and get bogged down with them while destiny is waiting.

Beloved we have a bigger task in the kingdom than to be tied down by doctrinal issues or wasting time responding to minor issues. Keep your focus on your calling and your destiny. You can choose not to respond to attack from within or without. Live in peace with all men. Goliath (the devil) is the enemy.

If it be possible, as much as lieth in you, live peaceably with all men. Rom. 12:18

Other's Comment

Precious London- When the voice of the enemy is coming through someone who dwells in your personal space, it can sound very loud; even louder than normal because that person is so close to you. But a loud threat doesn't make it any more real. The devils many tactics do not stop the fact that he is condemned to hell, as are his agents. Honestly, there is too much work to do in the Kingdom to be derailed. David didn't stop for long to try to figure out what Eliab meant from his comment. He continued on to do the work of the Kingdom. With the same spirit, I too am pressing on! Distraction will not steal my productivity! Amen.

Leshar Shaw- It certainly helps when you make a choice to see beyond the person speaking. The enemy is not coming as he is, he is coming through people to derail, distract, reject, set back , block and hinder. That is the devil's main goal, to take your focus off of Jesus and he will do it through any angle that he can get in. But thank God we are not ignorant of the devil's devices; we are moving forward regardless. As I was fasting someone kept trying to get me to eat but they didn't know that I was fasting and I didn't want to tell them. For a second I thought about eating and breaking my fast early but then I heard a voice say "Get behind me satan". After I heard that voice I had strength to continuously say no to eating! Thank God for the Holy Spirit.

Tremaine Nembhard- The reason the devil likes to take the opportunity to distract us using people closest to us, is quite simply because of the position they hold in our lives. These can be people whom we love, respect, and care about. Whose opinion are you going to give regard to more: your spouse or an old friend, or perhaps even someone you just met? What I found is key to perceiving and thwarting destiny distractions is the revelation, realization and total commitment to the goal/purpose/assignment/destiny. Jesus Christ was totally given to the assignment the Father had given Him. He was always talking of doing the Father's business, and was quick to cast down/rebuke anyone coming against the work. He had a thorough understanding of what must be accomplished. In Matt 6:23 satan even had the audacity to come through Peter. This is the same disciple that got the privilege to go on the mountain and see Jesus' glorified state. This was someone who walked very very closely with Him. But Jesus, praise God, still in tune to the heavenly assignment, was able to perceive and was quick to rebuke Satan, through Peter.

You can even take Job's wife. Job was a highly respected man before God, and was totally sold out to serving God. But guess who, when times got hard, told him to forget about God, to curse Him and die? His wife, his own flesh, the one who bore his children, made his home, cared for him and lay with him every night! But Job was a man who was totally given to serve his God and maintained his integrity.

Dazzling Buttcinn- Thanks for being a blessing. This message is timely. Keep the light shinning

Own Comment

____

____

____

____

____

____

____

____

____

Prayer:

My heavenly father, thank You so much for You are my Focus and my heart's desire. My mind is stayed on the You. I refuse to give in to the distractions of this life. Father I receive strength in my inner man to keep my eyes single. Great is my light in Jesus name.

HOLD FAST
DAY 26

That ye may be blameless and harmless, the sons of God, without rebuke, in the midst of a crooked and perverse nation, among whom ye shine as lights in the world; Phil. 2:15

Have you ever stepped into an environment that looks like everyone seems to be against what you say or are hostile to your belief? Some of us are being ridiculed for our testimonies and experiences in Christ.

The ungodly current around us is so strong that everywhere we turn to is like we are bombarded with temptations. From the market place, to the streets, to social spheres to political circles, it is becoming increasingly hard and tough to remain an uncompromising believer.

Beloved I will like you to be encouraged. You are not the only one the world is against. If Noah made it then you will surely make it too. Aren't you glad you are not even living in Noah's days because at least it is not the entire world that has lost it. Because then from neighbours to co-workers to partners everyone was completely soaked in the imagination of evil and wickedness. Can you imagine, God could not find anyone besides Noah and his family to save? It was a crazy world. (Gen. 6:6-8) Crazier than that was the world that Lot lived in and thank God you were not born in Sodom. Can you imagine a whole city coming together to sodomize two angelic strangers? (Gen. 19:4-10) They would not be deterred even after Lot pleaded and offered his two virgin daughters. What was that? That was a whole city sold out to unimaginable lust.

As a righteous person why would Lot ever choose to live in that kind of a city? The bible says his righteous soul was vexed. (2Pet. 2:5-8) Many of us are grieved daily by the things we see around us; ranging from crazy and heartless pursuit of sinful pleasures, under aged children with guns, children on the war front, father killing his whole family, betrayals of unimaginable magnitude, partners killing for insurance benefits and the list is endless. How could anyone enjoy that kind of world?

The bible says men loved darkness rather than light because their deeds are evil. (John 3:19) Beloved thank God you are not of this world. If the strong Noah made it and the carnal Lot made it out, by His grace you shall make it too.

"HOLD FAST" to the word of life, that is the key to shining in a crooked and perverse world. God noticed Noah, he made him a boat for his safety; God had mercy on Lot and whisked him out of that city and would not touch the city until Lot was clean gone.
Before this world goes up in smoke the Lord will come and take you out.

Other's Comments

David Foster- I like what you said about holding fast the word of life. Christ the living Word is likened to a rock that every builder must be build upon. Without the stability of the Word of Life you will struggle to stay in life. Christ who is our life is the only perfect anchor of our soul. Without holding on to the Word that is able to save us we will be lost. That light of life that we hold forth is the tool needed to push back the darkness in whatever area you may find yourself in. We are agents of change by the light that we shine because our battle is with darkness. Keep the Word close to shine bright.

Allison Khan- 2Peter 3:11 says 'Seeing then that all these things be dissolved what manner of persons ought ye to be in all holy conversation and godliness'. Being grounded in the Word is the only way to maintain your integrity in this world. Noah knew that he knew that he heard from God. If he didn't he would have easily been swayed by the mocking and strange looks that he got from neigbours and friends. Even Lot lingered after listening to his sons- in- law. But thank God for His mercy. The same flood that destroyed the world was the same flood that lifted up Noah and his family. The same Word and Saviour that the world is denying is the same One that shall lift us up if we endure until the end. Alleluia!

Amanda Foster- The degree of our shining is related to the degree of us holding on to the word. The Bible says hold fast, which means opportunities will arise for you to hold on to it. When God speaks, we should hear what He didn't say and said. Holding fast is an instruction because the Lord knows it might be tough, but the benefit is we are shining. Our elevation comes from holding the word. Holding the word will make us what it talks about. Whatever word we can successfully hold, we will successfully be. What the Lord is giving is not the material but it is the word in your spirit. Our forefathers really had it worse but they prevailed. Noah was the only one in the entire world, he had to be focused on the word. I love our forefathers, we definitely can learn from their choices. So I'll do what Noah did, because I saw the result.

Leshar Shaw-No matter what situation comes your way "the Word" is your way out and your only stability. You need a word to hold on to for every situation in order to come out like a shining light. The word was Peter's stability until he lost focus and dropped the word and then began to sink. When Peter dropped the word God in his mercy helped him up. God is still helping many believers up today. I really like what Amanda said about Holding Fast being an instruction because it is a must that in order for every believer to not lose focus by what's going on around them and have the victory in every situation you must hold the word tightly. It is more than possible to hold on to the word and not be a compromising believer. The only church God didn't have a problem with was Philadelphia, why? Because they kept the word (Rev 3:10). We are also in the family of them that keep the word!!!

Sarissa Ryan- Many situations have come my way where I'm stuck within the four walls of a school (not for long because I am almost finished), but the point is- if there is a wall in front of you God will see it and carry you like an eagle would on its wings.

Yvette Cameron-One particular scripture that helps to keep me Holding Fast is Matt 10:32-33 "Whoever acknowledges me before men, I will also acknowledge him before my Father in heaven. But whoever disowns me before men, I will disown him before my Father in heaven." In a generation and culture where the things of God are considered weird and the things that are weird are considered the norm one may even be tempted to "hide" so as not to stand out like a sore thumb. But this scripture always brings me back into perspective. It's okay to stick out like a sore thumb knowing that your name is being mentioned in the heavenlies because you refuse to stop mentioning His name in the earth. Favour in the heavens is better than any earthly favour we could ever receive.

Angel David-That ye may be blameless and harmless, the sons of God, without rebuke, in the midst of a crooked and perverse nation, among whom ye shine as lights in the world; Phil. 2:15. We live in a perverse nation but notice that its says, " ....among whom ye shine as lights in the world" But for your light to shine you have to have been holding on to the word. The word has to have been in you because Isaiah 60:2 says "For, behold, the darkness shall cover the earth, and gross darkness the people: but the LORD shall arise upon thee, and his glory shall be seen upon thee." When people put me down I look at it this way, my light is shining and shining because the world is going darker so that my light can lead them. I like what Allison said, Noah knew that knew that he heard from God or if not he would have been swayed. So when you have a personal revelation about God's word, it encourages you to continue to hold on. "Looking unto Jesus the author and finisher of our faith; who for the joy that was set before him endured the cross, despising the shame, and is set down at the right hand of the throne of God:" Hebrews 12:2 Jesus knew the glory of the throne so He knew being persecuted was joyous to Him as it should be for us. That we be counted worthy to be persecuted for his sake. :)

Own Comment

____
____
____
____
____
____
____
____
____
____
____

Prayer:

Heavenly Father thank You for Your word is life and truth. The word of the Living God dwells in my heart and lives in my mouth. In the name of Jesus I obtain mercy and grace to declare God's word till the very end.

DO NOT BE LIKE THEM
DAY 27

Be not ye therefore like unto them: for your Father knoweth what things ye have need of, before ye ask him. Math. 6:8

Religion tries to make God look like He does not care. Many of us grew up in a religious system where prayer is more about telling God about our needs. Jesus came to change that order by revealing God to us as a caring Father. Beloved, I don't know how many of you wait for your kids to tell you what they need before you know their needs. I know that sometimes we might not be in a position to meet our kid's needs but we certainly do know their needs. Our heavenly Father does not require you to tell Him about your needs because He knows them. So if we take out needs from prayer what is it about then?

Prayer is more of communion and fellowship with the Father. People who make needs the central point of their prayers will soon find reason to drop out from prayer meetings when their needs are met. With this kind of religious mindset, prosperity has stolen the prayer life of many.

As their need reduces their prayer life also reduces. The Lord said we shouldn't be like them.

And it shall come to pass, that before they call, I will answer; and while they are yet speaking, I will hear. ***Is. 65:24***

Comments

Precious London-God will meet you in the place of your own understanding. If we are constantly going to Him with requests, we will never have the opportunity to develop a relationship with Him. We cannot expect to go to Him with a million needs and then expect Him to manifest His glory to us also, when we haven't even taken the time to fellowship with Him. God's will is for us to pray continually, GIVING THANKS IN ALL CIRCUMSTANCES (1 Thes. 5:16-18). We must rest assured that as we are obedient to His will, He will remain mindful of our needs.

Leshar Shaw- Matt 6:33 doesn't say seek your needs first, it says seek the kingdom of God and His righteousness and everything else will follow. When you are committed to your spiritual needs you can be sure that your physical needs follow. The main reason we are saved is to have communion with God not for our needs to be met. God is not unrighteous, He is committed to providing for His children far more than we can imagine. It is complete bondage to be consumed with your needs. God is the God of liberty!!

Amanda Foster-

God desires fellowship, when our fellowship is only based on needs you find it's very shallow. When you are in relationship with people that take all the time or someone sensitive, you find it hard to be honest. That's not a relationship. We are blessed of the Lord when He can rebuke us and we enjoy it. We have the freedom with God. Fellowship is a private intimate place with the Lord, it's in there that we grow the most, because He can be honest about us and help us grow. The presence of God is to be valued, it is being with the Maker of the world.

Azhia Julien- Those whose prayers look like a grocery or to-do list, pray out of fear. That's like praying when you see a gunman coming your way; it's not time for prayer but for thanksgiving and praise because you just know that you know that you know that you have the victory in Christ and can't possibly get shot and die. God doesn't respond to fear. When you fear you're saying, God I don't trust in you.... I don't think you are able. And that is the opposite of fellowship. When you get into fellowship with the Father we are supposed to tell Him how great and faithful He is even if our circumstances tell us otherwise. That is called faith and that just so happens to be the only thing that moves God. Sure you cast your cares unto the Lord but as you get into His presence those burdens must be lifted and replaced with the fullness of joy.(Ps 16:11) Then it comes to maintaining His presence because in His presence is liberty (2Cor3:17) from worrying about needs. The presence of God is something that needs to be activated, and it's only activated when all focus and attention is on Him, not on ourselves.

Sarissa Ryan- Many people look to God as if He does not know what they are going through or what they need. So what they usually do is they will set a time apart to complain to God for what they do not have. Before I came to Christ House of Glory International, I was always told to pray to God for things I did not have and to let God know what is going on in my life like He could not see me. But now when I pray I realize that He is never far away and that He knows my needs.

Yvette Cameron-I like the idea of prayer being as you said "communion and fellowship with the Father". It makes it two-sided and not the one-sided communication we often see demonstrated in many Christian circles. Prayer often looks more like us throwing our "verbal fists" in the air, battling in prayer to get what we are praying for. But this idea of communion changes the whole perspective of prayer. It's all about FELLOWSHIP no matter what kind of prayer it is.

Own Comment

____

____

____

____

____

____

____

____

Prayer:

My dear heavenly Father, there is none holy and righteous as You are. I am glad my righteousness is of You and my needs are met by You. In the name of Jesus

Christ I receive grace and mercy to focus on You more than on my needs. Amen.

FOR THIS PURPOSE
DAY 28

But rise, and stand upon thy feet: for I have appeared unto thee for this purpose, to make thee a minister and a witness both of these things which thou hast seen, and of those things in the which I will appear unto thee; Acts 26:16

I don't know how well you will think of somebody who places a phone call to you without a reason. You will certainly not think well of the President of a country calling you on phone and when you ask, "Why are you calling me sir?" he replies, "I don't know."

There is nothing that God has done without a purpose. Whenever and if He appears to you He has a purpose. Never take His presence for granted, there is always a reason behind it. He appeared to Paul to reveal his calling as a minister.

Beloved your entire life has a purpose. You were created for an assignment. (Jer. 1:5)
Unfortunately, many of us define our purposes in life by our gifts and talents. Gifts and talents can be a good indicator but may not necessarily define your assignment and calling in the kingdom. You may have been gifted to cast out devils, work miracles, or even teach and preach

the word but that does not necessarily mean you are a Teacher, a Pastor or a Prophet.

Some of us respond to need and give ourselves assignments and expect God to back us up. The need in the land does not define your assignment either. Some of us like to do what others are doing because it pays them well. While some of us are just set up by our successful parents and turn ministry into a family business. (Though ministry can sometimes be a family business if the individuals involved are called) Some of us go from counselors to counselors to help define our assignment and role in life. While some others are just driven by a desire for fame and money.

Beloved I want you to know the HOLY SPIRIT is the main Worker in the vineyard and the Lord Himself is the Owner of the vineyard.

Comments

Precious London- It is very easy to confuse your gifts and talents with your purpose. One reason is that you are excelling in an area and so you think that you are "called" for that purpose, but I think that can also be a reflection of your faith. To use your gifts as an indication for purpose can inadvertently be a way of hiding under the strength of your own human abilities and not allowing God to stretch you in other areas and bring you into unfamiliar territories. As our gifts can open the door for us in many ways, we definitely have to hear from God as to where to go once we walk through those doors; our purpose in entering

Azhia Julien- Everyone on this earth has gifts and talents deposited in them. The children of the devil are using their talents to spread the message of his kingdom everyday. "...For he maketh his sun to rise on the evil and on the good, and sendeth his rain on the just and on the unjust." Math 5:45
Gifts and talents are just one of those things God so graciously gave to everyone to make a living on this earth. But it is only the called of Christ, (Rom1:6) that are called to glory. "Even every one that is called by my name for I have CREATED HIM FOR my glory..." Is43:7 AND that is our purpose.
Everyone has talents, which people refer to as their "strengths" But we all know that God loves to glorify Himself in our weakness. We can only find our purpose in the secret place of the Most High, where He reveals many things to us. That's why I find it funny when unbelievers say, "Oh I know my purpose in life." How can you know your "purpose", when you don't even know the One who appointed you?

Amanda Foster –"Whereunto I also labour, striving according to his working, which worketh in me mightily." Col 1:29 One thing I have learned is that you don't want to work outside the working of the Holy Spirit in your life. There is a purpose for our life, and whatever God has called us to do the grace and the anointing will be there. I can say from personal testimony I am locating my path not because of obsession to know, but because I want Christ. The presence of God is the number one key to your destiny, because it's all about Him. He is the Master Builder; and like any secular field where you have to go to the head for the blueprint, so it is for believers. Go to God for the blueprint of your life.

Allison-This message ought to liberate us as believers. No longer should we pursue the destination for our life but use our days to seek the Giver of life. It is God who works in us both to will and to do of His good pleasure. We need to spend time seeking His good pleasure not using time to do what we find pleasurable or doing what will bring us pleasure. Our only pursuit should be relationship and intimacy with the Father; everything else comes from that.

Sarissa Ryan -Many people are blind to what God gives them. It's like having a wooden stick in your eye and many people neglect to hear the voice of God to know where God wants them.

Yvette Cameron-It was Myles Munroe who said, "When the purpose of a thing is not known abuse is inevitable." When you don't know your purpose you more than likely will end up misusing/abusing your gifts and talents. Every product that is in this world comes with a manual. When God made us He also gave us a manual to guide us about our purpose and that is His Word. The number one thing of course being to know Him and fellowship with Him, everything else is secondary. As much as the Apostle Paul achieved, Philippians 3:8-10 tells us that Paul said, "I consider everything a loss compared to the surpassing greatness of knowing Christ Jesus my Lord, for whose sake I have lost all things. I consider them rubbish, that I may gain Christ...." Christ was his main focus and so should be ours, regardless of whatever else the Father may ask us to do in this life.

Own Comment:

____

____

____

____

____

____
____
____
____

Prayer:

Dear heavenly Father, I am so glad that You are a God of purpose and distinction. My life is designed for a purpose. Father I obtain mercy and grace to listen, hear and understand your will for my life in Jesus name. Amen.

OUR HEART'S LUSTS AND COUNSELS
DAY 29

But my people would not hearken to my voice; and Israel would none of me. So I gave them up unto their own hearts' lust: and they walked in their own counsels. Psa. 81:11-12

Studying the gospels, have you not noticed that Jesus and the Pharisees and the Sadducees are always at it? In fact we can act a drama of Jesus versus the Pharisees and Sadducees. The Lord was never friendly to the religious order of His days. Why should you be today? But one thing was obvious, He was close to the needy, the poor and the sinners. He was healing their sick, raising their dead and teaching the principles of the kingdom.

A bruised reed shall he not break, and the smoking flax shall he not quench: he shall bring forth judgment unto truth. Isa. 42:3

God our Father never gives up on people who seek Him, who love Him and who are struggling to find the path. His strength is available for the weak. He is hope for the hopeless and a sweet song for mourners. He is the Bread of life, the Joy of the Season. He will always be there for you and me. He told Jacob, "I will not leave you until you are blessed." (Gen 28:15)

The Lord has also promised to be with us till the end of the age. (Math. 28:20) This then makes us wonder what could have been wrong with them for Him to have given them up. How strong is the pull of ***'heart lust and own counsel*** that was so strong that God had to say, "Okay, I give up"?

Beloved the Spirit of God will not strive with man forever. (Gen 6: 3) Sometimes looking at events around the world, you cannot but wonder if God is still interested.

And even as they did not like to retain God in their knowledge, God gave them over to a reprobate mind, to do those things which are not convenient; Rom. 1:28

.... because they received not the love of the truth, that they might be saved. And for this cause God shall send them strong delusion, that they should believe a lie: 2Thes. 2:10-11

Beloved, may you never be found with 'your own counsel and heart's lust'. These are the most dangerous things you can ever possess because of their potentials to drag you away from God.

Acknowledge the Lord in all your ways, (Prov. 3:6) Set your heart and motives right always before Him. Seek

His counsel by daily communion with the word. The Lord is forever with you. Amen.

Other's Comment

Sarissa Ryan- God said, "I will never leave you nor forsake you." God is always on your side, God will get you through the obstacles that the wicked have thrown in your path. In everything that is going on in your life God wants to help you through and He will not stop until He has you fully, He doesn't want to leave anything out or leave anything unfinished.

Amanda Foster- What it all comes down to at this point is the heart. I love that scripture Isaiah 42:3, "A bruised reed shall he not break, and the smoking flax shall he not quench: he shall bring forth judgment unto truth." God is willing to work with the bruised if the bruised will work with God. The Pharisees knew Jesus was the Christ, but they didn't want to believe. Even when the guards reported His resurrection, they bribed them to cover it up Matt 28:12. That is a hardened stubborn heart, it's that kind of heart that causes God to take the back seat. When you know but don't want to know.

Allison Khan- Acts 13:46 'then Paul and Barnabas waxed bold and said, it was necessary that the word of God first have been spoken to you: but seeing you put it from you, and judge yourselves unworthy of everlasting life, lo we turn to the Gentiles.' When we turn aside from the word of God and from His counsel to follow after our own carnality, we are counting ourselves unworthy of this salvation. It's as if we're saying, no thank you to the abundant life Christ died for us to have. Eventually you stop offering the gift to someone who refuses to accept it.

Precious London-I have definitely noticed that as daily communion with the Lord increases, He reveals more and more areas where the counsel of your own heart can lead you astray. "The heart is deceitful above all things, and desperately wicked; who can know it?" (Jer. 17:9) The key to setting your motives right is in daily asking God to search your heart, purge it and bring your will into alignment with His will. Acknowledging the Lord in all that you do allows you to draw clear lines between issues of the heart and issues of the Kingdom.

Own Comment

____

____

____

____

____

____

____

Prayer:

Father thank You for giving me counsel and instructions. The Lord is my Counselor. By the Holy Ghost I get taught daily. The voice of the stranger I don't hear. In the name of Jesus Christ I receive strength to be obedient to the voice of the Holy Spirit.

KEEP MAKING AN IMPACT
DAY 30

Then answered one of the servants, and said, Behold, I have seen a son of Jesse the Bethlehemite, that is cunning in playing, and a mighty valiant man, and a man of war, and prudent in matters, and a comely person, and the LORD is with him.   1Sam. 16:18

There are many scriptures we read daily, which we sometimes overlook but which embedded within are some very important truths. Such is the above scripture. So many times we do great things for the Lord and think no one notices because it is not on the face of newspapers, internet or recognized by some authority we look up to.

When it was time for David to be brought to Saul and known in the palace, it took a servant of Saul to tell. One of the servants of Saul knew David as a 'mighty valiant man, a man of war, cunning in playing, prudent in matters.' You probably wonder how he knew that. Amazing! Long before David was ever known publicly as a mighty man of war, ever before he faced Goliath, a servant somewhere knew it.

Beloved you may not have been recognized yet as a public figure or by the so-called mighty of the land, but it so matters that your neighbours, your friends and those around you feel your impact. It matters that a little boy from across the street or an obscure person in the hinterland sees and tastes your grace.

Beloved, keep making your impact in your little corner of 'Bethlehem', and when it is time you will be celebrated and known on the mountain for who you already are in the valley.

Other's Comment

Amanda Foster- Whether big or small it's all for the Lord. Jesus has first called us to be His witnesses in Jerusalem, Judea, Samaria, and to the ends of the earth. Before we reach the ends of the earth it requires starting from our Jerusalem; our neigbours, friends and family. We are to have a lifestyle of reflecting Christ, it is that character that will cause us to shine and reach the ends of the earth.

Yvette Cameron- Luke 16:10 tells us whoever is faithful with little will also be faithful with much. Making our impact in the small seemingly insignificant place is our indication to God that when He gives us the bigger things we can handle it. It's often our passage way into the bigger things.

Precious London- Since December, I have been confessing Daniel 5:14 over my life: "They will hear of me, that the Spirit of God is in me, and that light and understanding and excellent wisdom are found in me." There is not much glory in being in church several days a week and then be known for a carnal/secular quality. The Lord said that by our fruits, they will know us. Our purpose is to be known for the light that we carry, not the routines that we carry out.

Sarissa Ryan-This is so true, many people give up in the belief that they will not get rewarded for what they do, but the little things like being kind, helping someone out, obeying your parents or just plainly doing what you know you are supposed to do pleases God. God does not want someone who thinks that they know it all. He is looking for those who are still child-like in their faith. Now don't get me wrong when I say child like, what I mean is that you trust in the Lord always, you always have faith and you aren't ignorant.

Own Comment

____
____
____
____
____
____
____
____
____

Prayer:

Father thank you for everything is naked before You. You are a God of Reward. My labour of love and seed of faith are all coming back to me. I receive grace to keep walking in love, in faith and doing good. Amen.

\---

WORSHIP WITH US AT

10-377 Mackenzie Ave. Ajax Ontario, Canada L1S2G2 www.chogi.org

FOR MORE RESOURCES VISIT OUR ONLINE STORE:

www.wix.com/rhomi77/5

www.rhomi.org

NEW RELEASE: GET YOUR COPY AT

www.wix.com/rhomi77/5 **or**
www.rhomi.org/2

Olu David
Recover And Succeed
What you need to know

www.ingramcontent.com/pod-product-compliance
Ingram Content Group UK Ltd.
Pitfield, Milton Keynes, MK11 3LW, UK
UKHW020220250726
13967UKWH00001B/104

9 781257 651160